The Lord's Prayer

BIBLE CLASSICS

The Lord's Prayer

SELWYN HUGHES

Published by CWR, Waverley Abbey House, Waverley Lane, Farnham, Surrey
GU9 8EP
Copyright © 2001 by Selwyn Hughes
First published in Great Britain 1986 in illustrated format. Revised edition
2001.
ISBN 1 85345 193 2
Design and typesetting: Christine Reissland and Elaine Bond at CWR
Creative Services
Printed in England by Linney Print
Photos: PhotoDisc, Digital Stock Corporation, PhotoAlto
Front cover images: PhotoDisc, Digital Stock Corporation

Unless otherwise indicated, all Scripture references are from the Holy Bible:
New International Version (NIV). Copyright © 1973, 1978, 1984 by the
International Bible Society.

Introduction

Sometimes, when a section of Scripture such as The Lord's Prayer becomes so familiar, we can become so caught up by its poetic beauty that we can miss the tremendous revelation that sits beneath the surface.

The Lord's Prayer remains one of the few shining beacons of light in a world that seemingly rejects intimate communion with its Creator. Church services continue to resound to this simple prayer and my conviction is that something wonderful is happening.

Some may view this cultural and spiritual ritual a quaint and possibly outmoded practice. However the great lesson on prayer by Jesus to His disciples still sings out its prophetic plea from a creation groaning for redemption by its Saviour.

I invite you to join me on a pilgrimage through The Lord's Prayer. It is my heart and prayer for you, that as we set off on our journey, that you come to a new place in your faith walk.

As we now seek to become prayerful disciples, asking that familiar question, "Lord, teach us to pray", expect to be provoked, blessed and challenged along the way. And be in faith that your questions will be met - not only with answers, but revelation of the great Teacher Himself.

Selwyn Hughes

Jesus
– pattern of prayer

The Lord's Prayer is surely one of the most precious passages in all the New Testament. As we set out to explore this remarkable text we can be confident that we are about to embark on a spiritually rewarding and stimulating journey. These words of Jesus, so seemingly simple, encompass every conceivable element in prayer and reduce it to a clearly understood pattern.

The Lord's Prayer (or, more correctly, The Disciples' Prayer) is, amongst other things, a miracle of condensation. In the short compass of 66 words (as found in the AV translation), the Master presents a model of praying that touches on every major aspect of prayer. One writer says of it, "The Lord's Prayer sets the standard for all praying. Everything every man ever needed to understand about prayer is latent in the choice disclosure of these words." That might sound like an astonishing claim, but it is true. No set of theological volumes, no sermon, no series of writings could ever capture the fullness of all that prayer is as does this simple yet profound model.

The more we understand this model, and the more we pray in line with it, the more powerful and productive our prayer life will become. All communication with God begins with prayer, and because this communication is so important, the enemy seeks to disrupt it. This is why we face the necessity to constantly refocus our thinking on the subject, and seek to deepen and enhance our prowess in the art of prayer. If the Lord's Prayer sets the standard for all praying, then we must lay our praying alongside His pattern in order that our prayers might become more and more like His.

Some Christians think that prayer consists solely of reciting the words of the Lord's Prayer, but, as the great preacher C.H. Spurgeon once said, "To recite the Lord's Prayer and believe that you have then prayed is the height of foolishness." This does not mean, of course, that there is no spiritual value in reciting it, providing we realize that it is not just a prayer to be recited. Personally, I would not want to deprive Christian congregations of the pleasure and joy of reciting together the Lord's Prayer, but I do want to encourage them to view it as a departure point rather than an arrival platform.

If Jesus advised His disciples to avoid "vain repetitions, Matthew 6:7-8 as the heathen do", would He then immediately follow it by giving us a prayer to simply recite? Obviously, as I have said, one can derive great spiritual pleasure from repeating the words that Jesus gave us, but if we are to obtain the greatest value from the Lord's Prayer, then we must view it as a skeleton on which we have to put flesh. If you view these words, not merely as something to recite, but as an outline from which you must work your way when praying, no matter what you are praying about, then you will experience a growing confidence that you are praying the way Jesus taught. You see, it's one thing to recite a prayer: it's another thing to know how to pray.

Suppose "Our" had been "My"

We now look at the first word with which the prayer begins – "Our". That first word determines the very nature of the Christian faith. Suppose it had been "My"? That would have changed the whole nature of the Christian religion. Instead of our faith being "our" centred it would have been "my" centred – and that would have started us off wrong.

Matthew 6:9 (RSV)

In the field of prayer, as in many other fields, to start wrong is to finish wrong. The word "our" involves a shifting of emphasis from me to the Father, and to my brothers and sisters in the Kingdom. It implies a renunciation – a renunciation of myself. We see something similar in the first words of the Beatitudes: "Blessed are the poor in spirit" (the renounced in spirit) "for theirs is the kingdom of heaven" (Matt. 5:3, NIV). All the resources of the Kingdom belong to the renounced in spirit. So, in the first word of the Lord's Prayer, we find an implied demand that we adopt an attitude of self-surrender – surrender to the Father, and to His interests, and the interests of others in His Kingdom. If we do this, then everything opens to us. If not, then everything is closed. The rest of the Lord's Prayer has no meaning, and dies if the "Our" is not alive.

Matthew 5:3 (NIV)

And what does this mean? It means that the "Our" must stretch beyond our own fellowship, local church or denomination to include the whole family of God – everywhere. We will never get very far in prayer unless we come to it prepared to sacrifice self-interest, and willing to merge into God's greater plan for the whole.

A family
within a family

We now move on to examine the second word which appears in our Master's model of prayer – "Father". In Christian circles the term "Father" is probably the most common term we use when addressing God, and rightly so, for this is the pattern Jesus set when teaching His disciples the art of effective praying. Prayer should always begin with the recognition that God is our Father. This raises the much debated question: Is God a Father to all men and women everywhere, or only to those who are committed members of the Christian Church? For many years now liberally-minded theologians have taught that God is everyone's Father, so we are all His children, and thus all brothers and sisters. This teaching, known as the universal brotherhood of man, makes conversion unnecessary, and puts to one side the redemptive sufferings of Christ on the Cross.

The Bible teaches that God is a Father in two senses. firstly, He is the Father of the human family by virtue of creation. Malachi 2:10 says, "Have we not all one Father? Did not one God create us?" (NIV). In Acts 17:28 Paul said, "We are God's offspring" (NIV). In the sense of creation, yes, God is our Father. In the sense of a familial relationship, He is not. Jesus said in John 8:44 to the Jewish leaders "You belong to your father, the devil" (NIV). Quite clearly, the fatherhood of God is seen in the Bible in two senses. He is the Father of all men and women because He is their Creator, but He has another family – a family within a family – consisting of those who have committed themselves to Jesus Christ, the Son.

This leads to the question: for whom was the Lord's Prayer designed – for everyone or only God's redeemed children? There is no doubt in my mind that it was intended for Christ's true disciples, those whose lives are entirely committed to Him and to His cause. Obviously many people outside the Christian Church find the words greatly appealing, but much of the appeal is sentimental rather than spiritual.

To understand the Lord's Prayer, and apply its principles in the way our Lord intended, one needs to have experienced a genuine conversion. Then, and only then, does its meaning become apparent. Jesus shows us in the first sentence of His prayer pattern that true prayer must begin with a concept of God as Father. Someone has pointed out that the term "Father" answers all the philosophical questions about the nature of God. A father is a person, therefore God is not an invisible force behind the machinery of the universe. A father is able to hear, therefore God is not an impersonal being, aloof from all our troubles and trials. And, above all, a father is predisposed, by reason of his familial relationship, to give careful attention to what his child says. When we pray, then, to the Father, we must hold in our minds the picture of our eternal Creator as a being who has a father's heart, a father's love and a father's strength. This, then, must be the second note we strike when praying – God is a Father, and we must come to Him with all the trust and frankness of a child. Otherwise it is not prayer.

Galatians 4:4-7

Also, it is not enough that we address God as "Father", simply saying the word with our lips. We must understand the nature of God's fatherhood, for if we don't, then we will never be able to pray in the way that Jesus laid down for us. I have said before that no one can rise higher in their prayer life than their concept of God. If you do not hold in your heart a picture of God as He really is, then your prayers will be short-circuited, and, like electricity when it has nowhere else to go, will run into the earth.

Permit me to ask you a personal question: what goes on in your thoughts and feelings when the word "father" is mentioned? Some will have positive thoughts and feelings like warmth, love, affection; while others will experience negative feelings such as remoteness, sternness, or even unconcern. For many people, the word "father" has to be redeemed or amended, because it conjures up memories of unhappy relationships. I believe that this is why Jesus, after laying down the structure of prayer in Luke 11, then went on to teach us, through the parable of Luke 11:5-13 the friend who came at midnight, just what God is really like. He is not only a Father, said Jesus, but also a Friend. Christ, knowing that for some the word "father" would have negative connotations, attempted to fill it with a deeper content, by showing that God was a Father and a Friend. We must make sure that our concept of the word

"father" is a positive one, for if it isn't, then we will never be able to approach Him with the confidence of a trusting child.

This principle is absolutely key, namely, that we will never rise higher in our prayer lives than our understanding and concept of God. Time and time again, I have watched Christians struggle over this issue. They ask God for things which in their intellects they know are right and proper, yet they fail to get answers to their prayers because, deep down in their hearts, they have a doubt about His willingness to respond to them. Their intensive praying on an intellectual level is cancelled out on an emotional level.

This is why, if we are to learn to pray the Jesus way, we must seek to develop a clear understanding of the fatherhood of God. But how can we gain a picture of God's fatherhood that is true to reality? We do it by focusing upon Jesus.

"The philosophies of India," said one great writer, "are the high watermark of man's search for God. Here the mind of man strained itself to search for God and speculate about Him. But in all their searching, they never discovered that He was a loving and tender Father. And why? Because they had no Jesus. They had Ram, Krishna, Buddha and many others, but no Jesus." That lack was the vital lack. For Jesus is the expression of the Father in human form. If you want to know what God is like as a Father, then gaze at Jesus. He drives the mists and misconceptions from around the Deity, and shows us that the heart that throbs at the back of the universe is like His heart – a heart overflowing with unconditional love.

Getting the
right focus

We turn now to focus on the second clause of our script: "who art in heaven". One of the wonders of Scripture is its ability to introduce us to vast themes with a minimum of words. In the Lord's Prayer, a library is compressed into a phrase; a volume squeezed into a single syllable. These inspired words and phrases have become the source of numerous writings and expositions, and none of them, this one included, can fully plumb the depths of all that our Lord was saying. We now ask ourselves: what was in our Master's mind when He taught His disciples to pray, "Our Father who art in heaven . . .?" He wanted to teach them (so I believe) the way to achieve a true perspective in prayer. Before we can pray effectively, we must first be convinced who God is (our Father) and where God is (who art in heaven). In other words, the initial focus of our praying should not be on ourselves but on God.

Doesn't this reveal at once a fatal weakness in our praying? We come into God's presence, and instead of focusing our gaze upon Him, we focus it on our problems and our difficulties, which serve, in turn, to increase the awareness of our lack. Perhaps this is the reason why, when praying, we frequently end up more depressed or more frustrated than when we began? This is perhaps one of the greatest lessons we can learn about prayer – the initial focus must be upon God. We must focus upon God before we begin to focus on ourselves. How many times, when making an approach to God in prayer, have we gone immediately into a series of petitions that have to do with our problems, our difficulties, our circumstances? And so, by focusing our attention on what is troubling us, we end up wondering whether or not God is big enough, or strong enough, to help us.

In the first six words of the Lord's Prayer, Jesus shows us a better way. He tells us to take a slow, calm, reassuring gaze at God – at His tenderness, His eagerness to give, His unwearying patience and untiring love. The result of this, of course, is that we develop a calmness and tranquillity in our spirit which means we will find it no longer necessary to plunge into a panicky flood of words.

In some parts of the world one can enroll in courses called "Imagineering" – courses that are designed to stimulate creative imagination. Most of our problems begin in the imagination – "One can never become proficient in prayer," said one great writer, "until the imagination has been redeemed." What did he mean? He meant that when the imagination is redeemed from self-concentration, sex-concentration, sin-concentration, and makes God its prime focus, then it becomes creative-conscious, since its attention is concentrated on the Creator and the Re-creator. And when the imagination is redeemed, all the doors of the personality fly open.

God's postal address

Moving on, we now ask ourselves: why did Jesus bid us pray, "Our Father who art in heaven"? What is so important about the fact that God lives in heaven? Someone has suggested that heaven is "God's postal address", and, therefore, the place to which all prayers and petitions ought to be directed. I believe, however, that Jesus, in using the words "who art in heaven", sought to focus our minds, not so much on God's location, but rather His elevation. We are so used to living, as we say, "in a man's world", surrounded by limitations and restrictions, that we are apt to forget that God exists in a realm where there are no shortages and no restraints. Here, on earth, we stagger from one crisis to another, face endless problems such as economic recessions, strikes, political unrest, and so on, but in heaven, where God lives, such situations are non-existent. There are no shortages in the factories of His grace, no disputes on His assembly lines and no faults in His communication system. Ring or e-mail "Calvary" at any

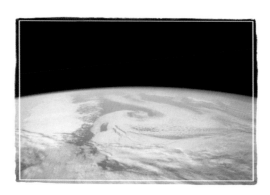

hour of the day or night, and you will be put into direct contact with the King of kings! Can you now see what Jesus means when He bids us focus on God who is in heaven? He is telling us to elevate our spiritual vision until it breaks free of earth's gravitational pull, and to remind ourselves constantly of the fact that, in our Father's presence, our greatest problems turn into possibilities.

The Saviour (so I believe) encourages us, when we come to God in prayer, to get our perspective right, and to look above "the ragged edges of time" to the heights of eternity where God has His royal throne. The old Welsh preachers and theologians such as Christmas Evans, Daniel Rowland, and others, used to call this aspect of prayer "settling down in God". They taught that when we gain a right perspective of God and heavenly things, then and only then, can we have a right perspective of man and earthly things. It was only when Isaiah saw the Lord "high and lifted up" that he was able to put into focus the events that were happening around him. Our life here on earth can never be abundant unless we realize that we have access to resources which are outside the realm of terrestrial things.

Isaiah 6:1-13

I have always said, that a good working translation of the term El-Shaddai (Gen. 17:1) is "God – the Enough". Actually, of course, He is more than enough, but how comforting it is to know that He is at least that. So, when coming to God in prayer, learn to settle yourself down in God. Remind yourself that His resources so infinitely exceed your requirements; His sufficiency so immeasurably surpasses every demand you may make upon it. Get the divine perspective right and earthly things will fall into their right and proper focus.

"Too close
to the ground"

Quietly we are coming to the conclusion that before we can see the events of time in their proper perspective, we must learn to focus our gaze upon God. The reason why our personal problems and difficulties seem so large and ominous is due mainly to the fact that we have not brought God into proper focus. When we see Him as He really is – "high and lifted up" – then all our troubles and anxieties are reduced to their proper proportions. A minister looked through his study window one day into the garden next door. He saw a little boy there, holding in his hand two pieces of wood, each about eighteen inches long. He heard him ask his mother if he could make a weather vane. After getting her

permission, he proceeded to nail one piece of wood upright on the low garden wall, then nailed the other piece loosely on top. Soon the loosely nailed piece of wood turned and twisted, first this way and then that, and the little boy danced with delight. He thought he had a weather vane that registered the winds, but all it did was register the draughts. "It turned half a circle," said the minister, "when the back door banged." From where the minister sat in his study, he could see a real weather vane on the church steeple. It was as steady as a rock in the constant winds that blew in from the sea. There are many Christians, however, who are like the little boy's weather vane – at the mercy of every gust of circumstance, their thoughts of God fluctuating with their personal experiences. They take their direction from a weather vane that is too close to the ground.

The Psalmist tells us that one way we can focus on the greatness of God is to consider His handiwork in creation. All around us in this wonderful world, we see evidences of His sublime sufficiency. Consider, for example, the vastness of the universe. Scientists tell us that in relation to the myriads of other celestial bodies in outer space, the planet we inhabit is like a tiny speck of dust in one of the huge London railway stations in relation to all the other specks of dust around it, or like a single grain of sand among all the other grains of sand on all the seashores of the world. They tell us also that if the earth were to fall out of its orbit, and spin away into space, it would create no more disturbance than the dropping of a pea in the Pacific Ocean!

Such word pictures, inadequate as they are, do, nevertheless, help us form some idea of the greatness and power of our God. Who can meditate on the vastness of the universe without experiencing an expansion in their conception of the majesty of God? I have often pondered on why God constructed the universe on such a grand scale, and my conclusion is this – He did it to show us that He is gloriously sufficient, unchangingly adequate and abidingly faithful.

A time exposure to God

Over the past few pages we have been seeing the futility of presenting our petitions and requests to God before pausing to reflect on His unchanging adequacy and sufficiency. We said that one reason why Jesus directed us to use the words "who art in heaven" was to encourage us to focus our gaze on a God who is unaffected by the restrictions and limitations of earth, and who dwells in a place where the resources never run dry. Those who plunge into the areas of petition and intercession, before reflecting on the abundant resources that lie in God, will find their praying ineffective. They are praying contrary to God's pattern. The poet says:

> *What a frail soul he gave me, and a heart*
> *Lame, and unlikely for the large events.*

However, I wonder if, more often than not, we haven't given ourselves "a heart lame, and unlikely for the large events" because we rush into God's presence to present our petitions before taking stock of our spiritual resources. God offers us infinite resources for the asking and the taking – Himself. The first moments of prayer should, therefore, be contemplative, reflective, meditative. As we gaze upon God and His infinite resources, we take, as someone put it, "a time exposure to God". His adequacy and sufficiency are printed indelibly upon us. No matter, then, what difficulties and problems face us – we are more than a match for them. The vision of His greatness puts the whole of life in its proper perspective. "We kneel, how weak – we rise, how full of power".

Honouring God's Name

We come now to the next clause in Jesus' pattern of prayer: "hallowed be thy name"(AV). We ask ourselves: what does it mean to hallow the Name of our loving heavenly Father? To hallow something is to reverence it, or treat it as sacred. It is derived from a very important word in the Bible (Greek: *hagiazo*) which means to venerate, set apart, to make holy. Does this mean that our veneration of God makes Him holy? No, for nothing we do can add to His qualities or attributes, and nothing we do can subtract from them. God is the only Being in the universe who needs nothing, or no one, to complete Him. To venerate God means to give Him the recognition He deserves, to acknowledge His superiority, and to treat Him with admiration and respect. This means that prayer is much more than a way by which we can talk to God about our problems and difficulties: it is a vehicle by which God can increasingly reveal to us who and what He is.

This might surprise some Christians who think of prayer merely as a means by which they can obtain things from God. Prayer, first and foremost, is a communication system through which God is able to reach deep into our spirits, and impress upon us His superiority, His power and His love. "I will do whatever you ask in my name," said Jesus. And why? "So that the Son may bring glory to the Father." If prayer does not begin by giving God a pre-eminent place in our hearts and minds, then it is not New Testament praying. Isn't it staggering that the first petition

John 14:13

in the Lord's Prayer is not on our own behalf but on His! Arthur W. Pink says in his book *An Exposition of the Sermon on the Mount*: "How clearly, then, is the fundamental duty of prayer set forth. Self, and all its needs, must be given a secondary place, and the Lord freely accorded the pre-eminence in our thoughts and supplications." This petition (hallowed be thy name) must take the precedence, for the glory of God's great Name is the ultimate end of all things.

So what does it actually mean to hallow God's Name? Are we required to pronounce God's Name in the quietest and most reverential of tones? Does it mean that we develop a mystical attitude toward the term God? No. In biblical times names were not just designations, but definitions. They had varied and special meanings. A name stood for a person's character, such as is demonstrated in 1 Samuel 18:30. "David behaved himself more wisely than all the servants of Saul: so that his name was very dear and highly esteemed." (Amplified Bible). The people did not esteem the letters of David's name. The statement means

that David himself was esteemed. We honour not just the Name of God, but also the characteristics that go under that Name. He is merciful, gracious, long-suffering, and so on. In other words, the Name of God is the composite of all His attributes. When we honour God's Name, we honour Him.

The ancient Israelites attached such a sacredness to the Name of God that they would not say it aloud. They thought that hallowing God's Name meant hallowing the Name itself. How utterly foolish and absurd! They paid honour to the actual letters of God's Name, yet, on occasions, thought nothing about disobeying His Word and denying His truth. One great Hebrew scholar points out that there is no such word as Jehovah in the Hebrew language, although it appears in English translations of the Old Testament. The Name of God in Exodus 3:14, where the Almighty gave His Name to Moses, I AM WHO I AM, is Yahweh: the English equivalent of which is Jehovah. The Israelites would not say the word Yahweh, and eventually the vowels were taken out and mixed with the consonants of another Hebrew word to form the word Adonai. This was done as a device to avoid having to say the real word "Yahweh". How ridiculous can you get?

Let us be quite clear, then, about what Jesus meant when He taught us to pray "hallowed be thy name". God's Name stands for who He is – His mercy, His compassion, His love, His power, His eternity, and so on. When, as God's children, we come to Him to honour His Name, we do more than enter into a religious routine – we contemplate all that His Name stands for, and reverence Him for what He is.

In line with God's character

We are seeing from our examination of Jesus' words in the Lord's Prayer – "hallowed be thy name" – that our first consideration, when approaching God, is the reverence of His Name. And why His Name? Because His Name stands for who and what God is. When we reverence His Name, we take into consideration all the ingredients of His character. The phrase "hallowed be thy name" implies that prayer is first and foremost a recognition of God's character and a willingness to submit to it. Jesus put first the determining thing in prayer – God's character. If our petitions are not in line with His character, then, however eloquently or persistently we plead our cause, the answer will be a firm and categorical, "No."

I wonder what would happen if we started our personal petitions with these words: "Father, if what I now want to ask You is not in line with Your character, then show me, for I don't want to ask for anything that does not contribute to Your praise and glory?" That would cause many of our petitions to die on our lips unuttered. Like the Mohammedan who washes his feet before going into the mosque, this attitude will wash our mouths, our thoughts, our desires, our motives. We would be saying, in effect, "Your character be revered first, before my desires or my petitions." This kind of praying puts God's character first and our claims second – putting both in the right place. True prayer, then, begins with God, puts self in a

secondary place, and seeks to honour and glorify God's
Name. It is characterised by a desire for God's will more
than our own will. Any other kind of praying is contrary
to Jesus' pattern.

Psalm 40:7–8

At this point we must ask ourselves an intriguing
question: why does Jesus, when laying down a pattern for
prayer, insist that our first consideration be the glory and
honour of God's Name? Is this a device (as some have
suggested) to appeal to the vanity and egotism of the
Almighty? Can it be that our loving heavenly Father wants
us to give Him what He wants (admiration and praise)
before He gives us what we want?

No, of course not! God encourages us to focus on Himself because He knows that in contemplating Him, we complete ourselves and bring all parts of our personality to health. To admire, appreciate, respect and venerate the character of God is to awaken ourselves to reality. Not to do so is to deprive ourselves and bring about a depletion of our powers. We were designed for the worship and contemplation of God, and when, therefore, we stand before Him and gaze at His majesty and glory, the machinery of our inner being whirrs into activity, and our characters take on the lineaments of His character.

God, therefore, has our interests at heart more than His own when He asks us to venerate Him. We "hallow" His Name and our own name (character) is hallowed. We gaze at His character and our own character is made better for the gazing. A shop assistant put it this way: "I just go quiet and empty into His presence, gaze at His glory and loveliness, and give myself time for His disposition to get through to mine." "Time for His disposition to get through." That's the secret. Give God a little of your time, and He will give you a little of eternity.

Not just a "Father"

We continue meditating on the phrase used by Jesus in the Lord's Prayer – "hallowed be thy name". John Calvin, one of the great theologians of a past generation, said of this clause: "That God's name should be hallowed is to say that God should have His own honour of which He is so worthy, so that men should never think or speak of Him without the greatest veneration." One of the things that saddens me about the contemporary Christian Church is the way that some believers refer to the Almighty in terms that drag Him down to a kind of "good buddy" relationship. They refer to the great God of creation as "The Man Upstairs" or "My Partner in the Sky". When people talk about God

in such low-level terms, they do Him an injustice. And it's not so much the terms, but the image of God that lies behind those terms which is the real problem.

We must, of course, strike a balanced note on this issue, as Paul teaches that the Holy Spirit in our hearts prompts us to call God, not merely Father, but "Daddy" (Rom. 8:15). Too much of the "Daddy", however, can lead us, if we are not careful, into sloppy sentimentalism. I believe this is why, after the phrase "Our Father", Jesus introduces us to another aspect of God – hallowed, holy, reverenced be His Name. It is right that we think of God in familiar terms such as "Daddy", but it is right also that we remember that our heavenly Father is a God of majestic holiness and unsullied purity. A. W. Tozer was right when he said, "No religion has been greater than its idea of God." Jesus put it into proper focus when He addressed God, not only as Father, but Holy Father.

John 17:11

A clear perspective

We have seen that hallowing God's Name does not mean having some kind of fetish about pronouncing the word "God" in hushed or reverential tones. It is rather hallowing all that God is, His qualities, His character and His attributes – all the things embodied in His Name. When the Psalmist in Psalm 102:15 said, "The nations will fear the name of the Lord," did this mean they feared the letters in the word "God" or "Yahweh"? No, they feared the Lord God Himself.

Psalm 102:15

At the risk of over-simplifying the opening clauses of the Lord's Prayer, what Jesus is teaching us is to come before the Father with this attitude: "Our Father, who cares for us with true tenderness, and who has in heaven the supplies to meet our every need; may Your attributes, Your nature, Your character, Your reputation, Your person, Your whole being itself be hallowed." This, then, is how prayer should begin. Before we start asking for what we want from God, we need to have the right perspective of God.

Gregory of Nyssa prayed: "May I become through Thy help blameless, just and holy. May I abstain from every evil, speak the truth and do justly. May I walk in the straight paths, sing with temperance adorned with incorruption, beautiful through wisdom and prudence. May I meditate upon the things that are above and despise what is earthly, for a man can hallow God's Name in no other way than by reflecting His character and bear witness to the fact that divine power is the cause of his goodness." Hallowed be the Name of God.

Thy kingdom come

We turn now to examine the fourth phrase in the Lord's Prayer: "Thy kingdom come". Jesus, after making clear that the first consideration in prayer is to focus on God's character, puts as the next issue the establishing of God's Kingdom. Any pattern of praying that does not make the Kingdom a priority is not Christian praying. Matthew 6:33 tells us: "Seek first his kingdom and his righteousness, and all these things will be given to you as well." If you seek something else first then your life will be off-balance.

Matthew 6:33

A newspaper once reported about a small town in Alaska where all the electric clocks were showing the wrong time. The fault, it appears, was in the local power plant. It failed to run with systematic regularity, and thus all the electric clocks were "out". When your loyalty and primary concern is for something other than the Kingdom of God, then everything in your life will be "out", too. One of the sad things about Church history is the fact that the Church has never really been gripped by the vision of the Kingdom of God. There are notable exceptions to what I am saying, of course, but, by and large, the Church has missed its way in this matter. One theologian points out that when the Church drew up its creeds – the Apostles', the Athanasian, the Nicene – it mentioned the Kingdom once in all three of them, and then only marginally. The Church will never move into the dimension God has planned for it until it puts the Kingdom where Jesus put it in this prayer – in a place of primary consideration and primary allegiance. I feel it is fair to suggest that the Christian Church down the ages has never really been gripped by the vision of the Kingdom of God. It has taught about it, of course, but it has never put the Kingdom where Jesus put it in His prayer, and given it the first consideration and the first allegiance.

Luke 12:31

"Thy kingdom come." Three simple words in both English and Greek, yet they open to us something so vast that one approaches them like a little boy standing on the seashore with a bucket in his hand wondering how to fit the vast ocean into his tiny pail! There is no way one can adequately and fully expound these words, but I hope I can whet your appetite over these next few pages, and then you can spend the rest of your life exploring all that is beyond them.

In the middle of the twentieth century the Church woke up to the fact that there was a missing note in modern Christianity – the Holy Spirit. Gradually at first, and very tentatively, the Church opened itself up to the Person of the Holy Spirit, and now there are comparatively few churches that have not been affected, to some degree at least, by His power and His presence. It seems strange, when we look back, that we could have remained content with a Holy Spirit-less type of Christianity. The same strange omission has taken place in regard to the Kingdom of God. There are signs that the message is being emphasised by certain groups and churches, but we are a long way from giving it the priority God demands. No wonder the Church has stumbled from problem to problem when its priorities are lost or only marginally held.

So it is, that despite the fact that Jesus taught us to keep the vision of God's coming Kingdom at the forefront of our prayers, the Church has failed, both in its praying and in its teaching, to give the truth of God's Kingdom the prominence it deserves. The Kingdom of God was the motif running through everything Jesus taught. However, I pick up many Christian books and magazines today and find that, with one or two exceptions, the Kingdom of God is not mentioned. Jesus made it the central note of His preaching and also His praying. It is time now to ask ourselves: what exactly does Jesus mean when He uses the word "kingdom"? The word "kingdom", *basileia* in the Greek, means "rule" or "reign". The Kingdom of God, then, is the rule or reign of God, His sovereignty, for which we are to pray. Jesus spoke of the Kingdom as being in the present as well as in the future. In Luke 17:21 he said, "the kingdom of God is within you." Wherever there is a heart that is surrendered to the claims and demands of Jesus Christ, there the Kingdom exists. But there is a day coming, says Jesus in Matthew 8, when both small and great will sit side by side in the Kingdom, and realise that in God's order of things there are no favourites.

Matthew 8:11

The Scripture tells us also that God has a Kingdom which is established in the heavens (Heb. 12:22–28), and the phrase we are studying "Thy kingdom come" – is a petition for God to let that Kingdom extend to every area of the universe where His rule is resisted. We are thus introduced to another great purpose of prayer – transporting to all parts of the universe, across the bridge of prayer, the power that overcomes all sin, all rebellion and all evil. We now need to ask ourselves: why is it necessary to have at the forefront of our prayers a vision of the Kingdom of God?

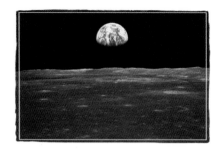

Philosophers have said that if we are to live effectively and securely in this world, then we must have a world view of things – a cosmic framework in which to live, think and work. The Germans call it *Weltanschauung* – the big picture. When we have a cosmic framework in which to think and work, then it gives a sense of validity and meaning to all we do. It makes us feel we are part of a universal purpose. Many modern thinkers believe that the reason why there is so much insecurity in the hearts of men and women is because there is a breakdown of that world frame of reference. One writer says, "Modern man is homesick. He is going on a hand-to-mouth existence day by day, and what he does and thinks does not seem to be related to the Whole. This has made life empty and jittery because it is insecure." The Chinese have a saying, "In a broken nest there are no whole eggs." The nest, the world in which we live and think and work, has been broken up by sin, and, therefore, our central unity has gone. This can be seen on a small scale when the home is broken. Invariably, behind every youngster living rough on the streets or in an institution, lies a disrupted home. Why? The framework in which they have lived has broken down and has left them inwardly disrupted and confused. As a consequence morals break down. Can you see now why Jesus taught us to have a world view of things? With our eyes focused on the Kingdom, we know that at the heart of things there is utter security.

In other words, it is crucial we see the "big picture". Could this be why Jesus, when laying down a pattern for prayer, taught His disciples to focus on the "big picture" – of the Kingdom of God? It could well be, but whether it is or not, one thing is certain – when we start off in prayer gripped by the certainty of God's coming Kingdom, our prayers are launched from a position of strength. I once remember a sales flyer that came in the post, and on it were the words: "Get the idea – and all else follows." I thought to myself, when the idea is God's idea, the Kingdom, then, indeed, all else follows. What if we were to begin our prayers, however, by focusing, not on the Kingdom of God, but on the kingdoms of this world? We would receive very little motivation from such an action. Man-made empires come and go. Egypt came and went. Syria came and went. Babylon came and went. Greece came and went. Historians tell us that at least 21 former great civilisations are extinct. Earthly kingdoms go the way of all flesh – the debasing power of sin, decay, distress and destruction is inevitable.

The Kingdom of God, unlike earthly kingdoms, is destined for success. Call it triumphalism if you like, but the eventual accomplishment of God's Kingdom has more reliability about it than tomorrow's dawn. When our minds are permitted to focus on such a tremendous truth, it will not be long, believe me, before the heart leaps up in confident, believing prayer.

Another kingdom

Although we have been focusing our thoughts on the Kingdom of God, we must not forget that there exists in the universe another kingdom – the kingdom of Satan. The Bible shows us that in the ages past there was just one kingdom, the Kingdom of God, but, through the sin and rebellion of an angel named Lucifer (now known as Satan), another kingdom was established over which the Prince of Darkness rules and reigns.

Every person, born into the world since Adam (with the single exception of Jesus Christ), comes under the dominion of Satan, and is, in fact, classified as a citizen of the devil's kingdom (Eph. 2:1–2). When, through conversion, we become followers of the Lord Jesus Christ, our citizenship is immediately changed, and we become citizens of the Kingdom of God (Col. 1:13). Once we receive this new citizenship whether we realise it or not, we are thrust into the front line of the age-long conflict which has existed between God and Satan, and we become participators in the Almighty's plan to bring about Satan's defeat, and to bring the universe once again under the control of God and His Kingdom. *Colossians 1:13*

Standing as we do on the cutting edge between the Kingdom of God and the kingdom of Satan, the Almighty has given us a weapon with which to fight, that is the most powerful in all the armouries of heaven. That weapon is prayer. Our citizenship in God's Kingdom entitles and enables us to pray, "Thy kingdom come". And when uttered with sincerity and trust, those words spell out, every time they are spoken, the ultimate triumph of the Kingdom of God.

We have already seen that one reason why Jesus taught us to focus on the coming Kingdom was in order to help us get our spiritual bearings, and thus be better equipped and fortified when praying for other things. Just as the mariner used to get his bearings from the stars to be able to put into the right earthly port, so we have to get our eternal values straight before we begin to concentrate on temporal things.

Nebuchadnezzar, lifted up by pride, was humbled and ate grass like one of the cattle until he realised that not he but God rules from heaven. Then he was restored to *Daniel 4:28-37* reason and to the throne. I am afraid that we will have to eat many of our words unless we learn that the heavens rule and the Kingdom of God has the last word. Oh that we could become so preoccupied with the Kingdom of God that it would affect every part of our being, our thinking, our working and our praying. Our own causes are valid only as they accord with the eternal cause of God. When I pray, "Thy kingdom come," I am really praying, "Lord, I pray that You will do whatever advances Your Kingdom, whatever brings in Your rule and Your reign." And, we might add – "even though my own 'cause' might have to be pushed aside." What a prayer! What a challenge! No wonder the ancient Jewish Talmud said that "the prayer in which there is no mention of the kingdom of God is no prayer at all". It's only when we get the Kingdom values straight that we can pray this prayer with assurance.

"Thy will be done"

We now come to the fifth clause in Jesus' pattern of praying: "Thy will be done, on earth as it is in heaven". It becomes obvious right away that if we are to know how God's will is to be done on earth, then we need to know how it is done in heaven. We ask ourselves, therefore: how is the will of the Almighty followed by the myriads of angels and other celestial beings who inhabit eternity?

Matthew 6:10
(RSV)

First, it is followed unquestioningly. There is no discussion or debate amongst the angels over any of the Creator's directives. Here on earth the Lord has to prod and poke in order to get His servants moving, but in heaven no such prodding is necessary. Second, it is done speedily. Once a command is received, then the angels move with the utmost speed to do His bidding. They eagerly wait for the next command so they can hurry to accomplish it. How slow and sluggish are we, His earthly servants, by comparison. Third, it is done completely. The angels carry out His bidding down to the tiniest detail. There are no alternatives, no omissions, no modifications to the divine orders. The will of God is done in fullest detail.

A little girl, seven years of age, asked me once, "Does an angel have a will?" I said, "I think so." "Then how many wills are there in heaven?" she asked. "Oh," I said, "there must be millions." "Wrong," she said. "There is only one. There were two once, but one got kicked out. Now God's will has full control." I was amazed at such clarity of thought from a seven-year-old. May the day soon dawn when the will of God is done on earth as it is done in heaven – unquestioningly, speedily and completely. We conclude then, that the angels respond to the will of God in unquestioning obedience and perform His bidding with the utmost readiness and willingness. Heaven can, therefore, be described as a totalitarian society.

We are rather afraid of that word here on earth as it brings to mind oppressive regimes where individualism is discouraged or repressed. I recognise that the word has negative connotations because of this, but, make no mistake about it, heaven is a totalitarian community. Those reading these lines who have had some experience of totalitarianism might say, "What! – are we to emerge from one totalitarian system to become involved in another?" The answer is yes. And God's totalitarianism is more thorough-going and absolute than any totalitarian regime on earth.

However, there is a profound difference. When you obey the will of God fully and completely, you find perfect freedom. When you obey other totalitarian systems, you find utter bondage, for they are not in line with the way you were designed to live. As the stomach and poison are incompatible, and when brought together produce disruption and death, so your being and "other-than-the-will-of-God" ways are not made for each other and produce disruption and death. However, as the stomach thrives on good wholesome food, and the two are made for each other, and bring health and life, so the will of God and your being are made for each other, and when brought together produce health, life and fulfilment.

John 8:34–36

We may dislike the word totalitarian because of its negative connotations, but we cannot get away from the fact that God demands total obedience; and because this is His will for humanity, then He desires the universe to be a totalitarian regime. However, as we said, it is a regime with a profound difference. When we obey completely the will of men, we find nothing but bondage. When we obey completely the will of God, we find nothing but freedom – perfect freedom.

There are many in this universe who think like Ephraim, of whom God complained, "Were I to write for him my laws, he would but think them foreigners' saws" (Moffatt). Ephraim felt that God's laws were foreign sayings or saws – something disruptive. But the will of God and the human will are not alien. They were made for each other. The expression is inadequate, but it is the best way I know of explaining the fact that my will functions best when it acts and behaves in accordance with His will. We must take hold of this until it becomes a basic axiom: my will and God's will are not alien. When I find His will, I find my own. I am fulfilled when I make Him my centre, I am frustrated when I make myself the centre. And if you are afraid that this depletes you as a person, or makes you into a cipher by subduing your individuality, then your fear is quite groundless. You are really at your best only when you are doing the will of God. Then all parts of your personality are drawn to health, vitality and fulfilment.

Forced to face reality

We continue for a moment meditating on the phrase: "Thy will be done, on earth as it is in heaven". Whenever we pray, we are to pray in accordance with God's will. One Greek scholar says that the words can be paraphrased in this way: "Your will, whatever You wish to happen, let it happen – as in heaven so in earth." In other words, "God, do what You want." It's not easy to pray this way. If anyone thinks it is, then it is probably because they have never really sounded the depths of self-interest within their own hearts.

It's hard sometimes to pray, "Thy will be done," when we know that if God has His way, we will not get our way. Has that ever happened to you? The basic reason for this conflict is due to the major problem of the human heart – self-centredness. Paul, when describing a self-centred life and its results in Romans 6:21, ends by asking this question: "Well, what did you gain then by it all? Nothing but what you are now ashamed of!" (Moffatt). The end was zero. That is the inevitable end of a self-centred life – nothing. The major thing that stands in the way of God performing His will in our lives utterly and completely is just that – self-centredness.

Romans 6:21

Did Jesus know that when His disciples prayed this prayer, "Thy will be done", it would sometimes produce a conflict within them? In my own mind, I am sure He did. He nevertheless framed the statement because He knew, as we now do, that if we are to become effective in prayer, then we must face up to the question: whose will comes first – mine or God's? I must be willing to say, "God, do what You want". That is the bottom line in prayer.

We cannot avoid the fact that this type of prayer sometimes creates a conflict in us, particularly at such times when we know that God's will is the opposite of what we ourselves want. We, then, must consider whose will is to have precedence – ours or God's? There are some Christians who pray, "Thy will be done", but they do it with a wrong attitude – an attitude of rebellion and resentment. They believe that they cannot escape the inevitable, and they become angry about it. When they say the words, "Thy will be done", they are almost said through clenched teeth. Other people say the words, not necessarily out of resentment, but with an attitude of passive resignation. They say the words, "Thy will be done", but what they mean is something like this: "Lord, I'm not very happy about the way things are turning out, but I suppose You know best. So I'll go along with it, and try my best to believe it's for the best."

The proper attitude to the will of God, and the goal for which we should aim, is one of rejoicing. It's not easy to arrive at such an attitude, I know, but nevertheless we must have it before us as the desired end. David prayed that way, and so, on occasions, did others in the Scriptures. If we can cultivate that attitude as the normal and characteristic reaction to everything that happens around us – sorrow, disappointment, disillusionment, frustration, disaster, loss, bereavement – then such a spirit is more than a match for anything. As someone has said, "The Hallelujah of triumph is louder than the Amen of resignation." It is!

Psalm 40:8

Down to earth

We now ask ourselves: what does Jesus mean by the term "on earth"? Theologians have argued for centuries over the preposition used here. Some say it should be "in" earth, and others say it should be "on" earth. I think that the word "on" is the truer translation, but I take the point that some theologians make when they say, "The phrase 'in earth' more nearly expresses the meaning than 'on earth' because God's ultimate will is destined to triumph not only over the minds of men, but over the disharmony and dissolution that is inherent in planet earth."

Paul put his finger on this issue when, speaking by the Holy Spirit in the passage in the book of Romans, he says, "The whole creation has been groaning." Who can doubt it? Despite the beauty of this glorious creation, everything that lives is subject to decay, disease and death. Life seems strangely poisoned near the fount. The lady who wrote the hymn "All things bright and beautiful" was only looking at some aspects of creation. She was being selective. She wasn't seeing nature "whole". But Paul did! If you place your ear to the ground (I speak metaphorically, of course), you will hear the groan of a creation that is crying out to be delivered from the effects of sin. But be assured of this – there is a day coming when the will of God will impose itself, not only "on" the earth, but "in" the earth, and will restore this sin-affected planet to its original beauty and majesty.

Romans 8:22

Most commentators believe the phrase "on earth" has reference to the world of human beings who have their home on this earth. In other words – us. Fantastic as it may sound, a day will dawn when this earth will be peopled with those who will do the will of God, not with resentment or resignation, but with rejoicing. That day may not be as far distant as we may think, so we ought to double our efforts in prayer, and joyously become involved in bringing our lives in line with His will. One thing is sure – the more you and I conform to His will, the more quickly can His purposes for this earth be realised. I have quoted many times the famous words of John Wesley who said, "God does nothing redemptively in this world except by prayer." Can you see what he is saying? The purposes of God for the future will have to cross the bridge of prayer. This raises the question: how committed are you and I to doing the will of God? Are we hindering or are we promoting the interests of His future Kingdom? It is vital that we Christians, both individually and corporately, focus our prayers on this issue with fervency and passion, remembering as we do so that the more abandoned we are to the divine will, the more speedily will His purposes come to pass for the world.

A change of focus

The Lord's Prayer falls naturally into two divisions: the first division focusing upon God, and the second division focusing on ourselves. We come now to the second part of the prayer, the part which has to do with our physical, psychological and spiritual needs. This natural division once again reinforces the truth we have been seeing, that it is only when God is given His rightful place that we can have the proper perspective towards ourselves. Jesus begins this part of the prayer by encouraging us to petition God for our physical needs: "Give us this day our daily bread".

Some Christians believe that it is inappropriate for most of us who live in the Western hemisphere to give expression to these words, as, they say, our problem is not so much where do we get the next meal, but how do we keep from eating the next meal! In an overfed, overweight society, so they say, our prayer ought to be: "Lord, teach us self-discipline, and prevent us from eating more than we need." At first glance, the phrase which Jesus used – "Give us this day our daily bread", does seem somewhat inappropriate, at least for those of us who live in Europe or North America. This prayer might be better uttered by the inhabitants of India, Cambodia, or some of the countries in Africa. However, to take that view is to misunderstand the deep truth which Jesus wants us to absorb. He invites us to pray, "Give us this day our daily bread", because when we say these words with sincerity and meaning, we build for ourselves a barrier against ingratitude. All that comes from God must be taken, not for granted, but with gratitude.

Matthew 6:11
(RSV)

Before we enlarge on this point, permit me to ask you a personal question: do you pray daily for your physical needs? Do you ask God daily for things like food, shelter and the other physical necessities of life? I must confess that when I asked myself that question, I had to admit that I did not. Now I have made a decision to apply myself to this part of the Lord's Prayer with greater sincerity and meaning.

Of course some people argue that because Jesus said, "Your Father knows what you need before you ask him" (Matt. 6:8, NIV), then it is pointless to inform God of our physical needs. He knows them already – so they say. Here we touch the central value of prayer. Prayer is not something by which we inform God of our needs, and thus influence Him to give things to us. Prayer is designed to influence us – it is we who are in need of this kind of prayer, not God. Of course God knows what we are in need of, but He also knows that unless we come face to face daily with the fact that we are creatures of need, then we can soon develop a spirit of independence, and withdraw ourselves from close contact and fellowship with Him. Prayer, then, is something we need. God may not need to be told, but we need to tell Him. That's the point. And unless we grasp it, we can miss the primary purpose of prayer.

To understand the truth of this statement we must ask ourselves: what happens when we neglect to pray for our daily needs and thank God for providing them? If we are honest about it, and examine our lives over a period of time, we will discover a subtle change taking place in our feelings and in our thinking. If we neglect to pray for our needs, we will begin to take the blessings of life for granted, and gradually, without at first realising it, we will succumb to the senseless notion that we can provide for the necessities of life, and that we are perfectly capable of managing our own affairs, without any help from God.

When we think that way, it is not long before pride steps in, and a kind of spiritual blindness settles upon us – a blindness which blocks our vision in relation to God, ourselves and others. We need, therefore, to constantly remind ourselves that everything we have comes from His hand, and that, at any moment, should He choose to do so, He could turn off the supplies, and we would soon become beggared and bankrupt. The only way, therefore, that we can build a barricade against this awful blight of ingratitude is to pray daily, remembering, as the poet said:

Back of the bread is the snowy flour,
And back of the flour, the mill,
And back of the mill is the field of wheat,
The rain, and the Father's will.

"They shall be satisfied"

We should by now be grasping, that the reason Jesus directs us to ask God for our daily bread is not because God has a need to know, but because we have a need to ask. It does us good to ask, for by asking we increase the awareness of our dependency upon God, and build a defence against the blight of ingratitude.

I find it greatly encouraging that the God of creation, who is infinitely holy, and who holds the universe in His hand, cares that my physical needs are met. This implies that God regards our bodies as important. He designed them and engineered them, and is interested in the way they function. Some Christians regard it as "unspiritual" to pray about the needs of the body, but, as Jesus pointed out, this is really where our personal petitions ought to begin. While Jesus endeavoured to get His hearers to keep their values straight, by saying that the spiritual was all important – "Seek first his kingdom" – He nevertheless put the body in its rightful place, as being a matter of great concern. The Father, we are told, guarantees our physical needs if we seek first the kingdom of God.

Matthew 6:33

Most of the promises in the Bible have to do with
spiritual truth, but never to the exclusion of the physical.
How much spiritual use would we be to our heavenly
Father if He didn't meet our basic physical needs? This is
why I do not fear the future. However men might
mismanage the resources which God has placed in the
earth, I have confidence in the truth of the Psalm: "in the
days of famine they shall be satisfied" (Psalm 37:19 AV).

The question being considered from several different angles in this section is this: Do we thank God daily for His provision for the physical necessities of life? Some might respond to this by saying: "But we never eat a meal without saying grace or giving thanks." Ah, but are you really thankful? Do you look up into your Father's face at least once every day, acknowledging that He is the source of everything, and giving Him thanks?

The term bread is regarded by most Bible teachers as a broad term for food. Just think for a moment what God has provided in the way of nourishment for His children. He has provided food in the grains of wheat, barley and so on, and, according to Genesis 43:11 and Numbers 11:5, He has provided nuts, vegetables, melons, and a whole host of other things. Keep looking in God's pantry and you will find food plants such as grapes, raisins, olives and apples. In addition to this, there are animals which provide food, such as oxen, sheep and goats, as well as different kinds of fowl. Then there are fish, and according to Leviticus chapter 11, even four types of insects! How thrilling is His bountiful provision. You and I eat nothing that did not come from the earth, and every element in it is the work of the creative hand of God. Not to recognise that is indeed the height of ingratitude. As the old hymn so aptly puts it:

Its streams the whole creation reach
So plenteous is its store.
Enough for all, enough for each,
Enough for evermore.

Pensioners of providence

We continue meditating on the ability of God to meet the physical needs of the human race. The thought of it staggered one scientist. "On this earth," he said, "with its diameter of 7,800 miles – a trifle too large to play with! – God is keeping in His charge some four billion black-haired or light-haired, two-legged vertebrate animals. What a family – yet He feeds them all."

There are many difficulties and problems facing us today in relation to economy, but the issue is not really that the earth cannot provide enough food. If there is a failure, it is a failure of distribution, not a failure in production. The food is there, but it is not properly apportioned. The former Prime Minister of India, Mrs Gandhi, once said that there are enough resources in India to feed that nation entirely, and then export two-thirds of what it produces. How wrong it is to blame God for the fact that thousands of people die of starvation each year. The fault is not in Him, but in us. God has given us His gracious promise: "As long as the earth endures, seedtime and harvest, cold and heat, summer and winter, day and night will never cease".

Genesis 8:22

As Isaac Watts puts it in his grand old hymn:

Thy providence is kind and large,
Both man and beast Thy bounty share;
The whole creation is Thy charge,
But saints are Thy peculiar care.

Is it not so? Yet how slow we are to pause and reflect that we are, in fact, literally the pensioners of providence!

We must spend one final moment considering the bountiful provision of our great Creator. A modern writer tells how once he asked an old man how he managed to live alone in a single cottage, miles from anywhere. The old man answered cheerfully that he enjoyed it since, as he explained, "Providence is my next-door neighbour."

Despite what many politicians and scientists tell us, the problems of this earth are not physical but spiritual. It is not over-population that requires our attention, but spiritual ignorance. If people came into a knowledge of Jesus Christ as their Lord and Saviour, then they would be given the insight and wisdom on how to use the earth's resources in the right manner. Murray Norris in his book *The Myth of Over-population* says that only fifteen per cent of the arable land on the globe is being farmed, and only half of that every year. It goes without saying, of course, that although God supplies the basic necessities, man has to put some effort into harvesting them; but, I say again, our problem is not lack of resources, nor too many people – it is our lack of dependency upon God.

Paul says when writing to Timothy, that God has created all food "to be received with thanksgiving by those who believe and who know the truth". Can you see what this verse is saying? God has provided an incredible abundance of food that we might express our thanks to Him. The rest of the world indulges with little gratitude. Let's make sure that not one day passes without this prayer meaningfully crossing our lips: "Give us this day our daily bread."

1 Timothy 4:3

Follow the pattern

We consider now the second petition of that part of the Lord's Prayer which focuses on us: "And forgive us our trespasses, as we forgive those who trespass against us". I use the word "trespass" (as found in *The Book of Common Prayer*) in preference to the word "debt", as in our modern society the word "debt" has come to have a monetary significance, and, by reason of this, has become somewhat narrowed. The word "trespass" has a wider significance and implies an offence done against another – an intrusion into someone's rights.

This second section of Jesus' pattern of prayer takes in every level of human life: the physical, the psychological and the spiritual. "Give us this day" refers to the physical part of life. "Forgive us our trespasses" has to do with the psychological part of life (the emotions, the thoughts and the will), and "Lead us not into temptation" has to do with the spiritual part of life.

Matthew 6:13 (RSV)

With characteristic accuracy, Jesus puts His finger squarely on the paramount need in human life. If we understand the Lord's Prayer correctly, there is really nothing more to be said when we come to this matter of prayer. This does not mean, of course, that, prayer has to be limited to these statements of Jesus, but it does mean that the issues He deals with, although we can expand upon them, cover the entire gamut of human need, and are the pattern for all adequate and effective praying. When we fail to cover the issues raised in Jesus' pattern of prayer, expanding on them in our own words, we deny ourselves the true power that lies in prayer. Follow the pattern and you find the power.

We now need to ask ourselves a pointed question: what is the biggest single problem which faces us in human life? Some would say ill-health; others, lack of money; still others, uncertainty about the future, or fear of dying. My own view is that the biggest single problem, with which human beings have to grapple, is the problem of guilt. A sense of guilt is the most powerfully destructive force in the personality. We cannot live with guilt, that is, truly live.

When I was a young Christian, I heard some great preaching in my native Wales, most of which focused on how God was able to release us from the guilt of inbred sin. Nowadays, apart from a few exceptions, that message is hardly heard in the pulpits of the Principality, or, for that matter, in many other pulpits in our land. The emphasis ceased to appeal to the modern mind, and so was discarded. However, it is now coming back through the science of psychology. Someone said that the point at which psychology and religion meet is at the point of guilt. Christianity and the social sciences underline what the human heart knows so well – it cannot live comfortably with guilt. In this simple prayer of Jesus, however, we have an adequate answer: "Forgive us our trespasses, as we forgive those who trespass against us." If we have fully accepted the forgiveness of God, and we know that our sins have been forgiven, then the result is a pervading sense of peace. The human heart cannot be put off by subterfuge: it needs reconciliation, forgiveness, assurance.

There are some pagan psychiatrists who take the attitude that guilt, being dangerous to the personality, must be dealt with by persuading their clients that there is no basis for their guilt feelings, that conscience and the moral universe are man-made concepts, and must be eliminated.

There is nothing, they say, to feel guilty about, so, as some put it: "Let bygones be bygones and wave goodbye to guilt."

It must be acknowledged that some ideas regarding guilt have to be dealt with in that way, for some guilt is false, and needlessly torments many sincere people. However, I am not talking here about false guilt. I am talking about real guilt – the guilt that the human heart carries because it has offended a holy God. You cannot get rid of that by waving your hand and saying: "Let bygones be bygones." Nor can you get away from sin by joking about it. Oscar Wilde said, "The only way to get rid of a temptation is to yield to it." But you do not get rid of temptation by yielding to it. It becomes an act, and then a habit and then part of you. No, we are hedged in – thorn hedges on either side. The only open door is the mercy of God. And these thorn hedges are His provision, too. They are God's creation enabling us not to live comfortably with evil, for evil is bad for us. God has so arranged the universe that we can only be truly comfortable with that which is good for us. I say again, guilt cannot be banished by subterfuge. Only God can redeem our wickedness.

The young doctor in A.J. Cronin's book *The Citadel* found his inner problems were revealed. When politics defeated his proposed health measures in a Welsh mining town, he sold his standards for money. After his wife's tragic death, he found in her handbag snapshots of himself taken during his crusading days. It reminded him of the man he might have been. He knew his pain was deserved, and he shouted at himself in a drunken stupor, "You thought you could get away with it. You thought you were getting away with it. But . . . you weren't."

You cannot get away with guilt, either by waving goodbye to it or by bottling it up within you. It "reveals" itself in your face and in your manner. Lady Macbeth, in Shakespeare's play, said, "What, will these hands ne'er be clean? Here's the smell of the blood still. All the perfumes of Arabia will not sweeten this little hand." Only the blood of Jesus Christ can erase the stain of guilt upon the human heart. When we pray, "Forgive us our sins," we are asking for the reality that God promises to everyone who asks of Him. And the only way we can fail to experience it, is simply not to ask.

The divine example

We have been meditating on the need for divine forgiveness, but it is time now to focus on the fact that Jesus adds a condition to this statement. He says that we can only ask God to forgive us our trespasses when we are willing to forgive those who have trespassed against us.

Matthew 6:14–15 (RSV)

Does this mean that before we can be converted to Christ, and have our sins forgiven, we have to search our hearts in order to make sure that we hold no bitterness or resentment against anyone? No. There is nothing in the Scriptures that states that a non-Christian receives forgiveness from God on the basis of claiming to forgive everyone else. Jesus is referring here, so I believe, to those who are His followers. They have been forgiven for their sins, but they now need a principle by which they can deal with guilt that arises, subsequent to conversion, through the violation of some biblical standard or commandment.

Paul says in Ephesians, "In him we have redemption through his blood, the forgiveness of our trespasses, according to the riches of his grace" (RSV). Grace – that's the basis of our forgiveness when we first come to Christ. But although we have received that forgiveness, we can never enjoy freedom from defilements in our Christian walk unless we are ready to extend the forgiveness God has given us to those who have hurt or offended us. This is an extremely important and serious issue, and one that we must not treat lightly, for if we fail to forgive those who have offended us, we break the bridge over which God's forgiveness flows into us.

Let's cover this key principle once again – if we are to keep clear of the problem of guilt in our Christian life, and experience divine forgiveness for our misdemeanours and sins, we do so only as we extend forgiveness to those who have offended us. That cuts deep. Perhaps you might be saying at this moment: "But I can't forgive: I have been

Ephesians 1:7

hurt too deeply." Then, may I say it very tenderly, but very solemnly, you can never, never be forgiven. "But if you do not forgive men their trespasses," says Jesus, "neither will your Father forgive your trespasses" (Matt. 6:15, RSV). In refusing to forgive others, you break the bridge over which you yourself must pass.

Matthew 6:15 (RSV)

A man once said to me, "I know I'm a Christian, but someone did such an awful thing to me that I find I can't forgive him." After spending a good deal of time with him, and getting nowhere, I said, "If it is really true that you can't forgive this person, it suggests that you yourself have not been forgiven, and you may be deluding yourself that you are a Christian." He looked at me aghast and went white in the face. My counselling methods are not always as abrupt as that; however, this brought him face to face with reality – and it worked. He got down on his knees, right where he was, and said, "Father, because You have forgiven me, I offer Your forgiveness and my forgiveness to my brother who has offended me, and I absolve him of his offence in Jesus' Name." Then what happened? Instantly the joy of the Lord streamed right into the centre of his being, and he laughed and laughed, literally for almost an hour.

I cannot over emphasise the important issue of extending the forgiveness we have received from God, toward those who have hurt us or trespassed against us. We must once again get to the root of this. Some say, "I can forgive, but I can't forget." But you don't really mean that, do you? See how this statement from the Lord's Prayer looks when set against that attitude: "Father, forgive me as I forgive others. I forgive that person, but I won't forget what he did. You forgive me the same way. Forgive me, but don't forget my sins, and when I do something wrong, bring up the whole thing again." God cannot, and does not, forgive that way. He blots the offence out of His book of remembrance. So must you. Perhaps you say, "Well, I'll forgive, but I'll have nothing more to do with that person." Now pray the Lord's Prayer with that in mind. "Father, forgive me as I forgive others. I forgive that person, but from henceforth I'll have nothing more to do with him. You forgive me in the same way. Forgive me, but have nothing more to do with me." You see its absurdity?

Isaiah 43:25

Don't try to forget things, don't try to smooth them over, and don't drive them into the subconscious. Get them up and out. A woman visited her doctor and asked him to give her a special ointment to smooth over her abscess. When the doctor refused, and said it must be lanced, she left his surgery and went home. In a few days the poison had spread through her system and killed her. Unbelievable? The lady was known to me. I beg you, when facing the issue of forgiveness, don't ask for a Band-aid or a halfway measure. Get it out. Forgive.

A knotty problem

W̶e move on now to examine the third petition in that part of the Lord's Prayer which focuses on ourselves: "Lead us not into temptation, but deliver us from evil". The first part of the Lord's Prayer relates, as we saw, to God and His glory. The second part relates to man and his needs. Here, in this third petition relating to our needs, the vital core of human need is touched, as Jesus characteristically puts His finger on the deepest need of the spirit – deliverance and protection.

An immediate problem, however, presents itself in these words, and it is one over which theologians have debated for centuries. The problem is this: if temptation is necessary to our growth (as we grapple – we grow), are we really expected to pray that God will not do what He must do in order to accomplish His work within us? After all, we are told, Jesus was led by by the Spirit into the wilderness to be tempted by the devil.

Mark 1:12-13

Over the years I have had more letters about this particular issue than probably any other subject. A letter that came a while ago put the problem like this: "If, as I understand it, the word temptation [Greek: *peirasmos*] means a test or a trial, why should we pray to be kept from it, particularly as James tells us to 'count it all joy when you fall into temptation.'" You see the difficulty I am sure. There are a number of interesting answers to this question, which we shall look at soon. As this is one of the most confusing issues in Scripture, we need to approach it with a good deal of dependency on the Holy Spirit so that He might illuminate our minds, and guide us into all truth.

So let us now examine some possible answers to the dilemma presented in the words, "Lead us not into temptation, but deliver us from evil" – namely, why should we ask God to keep us from something that could work for our good?

One answer to this problem is that Jesus, when using these words, meant not just temptation but unrecognised temptation. The advocates of this interpretation say that when temptation is recognised, it can be resisted, and when it is resisted, it then becomes a source of strength and power in our lives. One writer, who holds to this interpretation, put it this way: "If I am filling out my Income Tax form, and I know that some income has come to me through other than the usual channels, and there is no way of anyone checking it, I am confronted with a temptation to omit it. But I know that is wrong. No one has to tell me. I know it. And when I resist the temptation, I find I am stronger the next time, when an even larger amount may be involved."

There is a good deal of merit in this interpretation, for there is no doubt that evil can be more effectively resisted when it is clearly recognised. Simon Peter is an example of this. Jesus said to him in the Garden of Gethsemane, "Watch and pray so that you will not fall into temptation." Matthew 26:41 He did not heed that word, and became involved in a serious act of violence. Peter thought he was doing the right thing, but really his act of violence was due to his John 18:10 inability to recognise what was happening.

If we pray for the ability to recognise temptation when it comes our way, then we will be able to confront it, and turn it to advantage. Another interpretation of these words of Jesus is that this is a prayer for us to be kept back from more temptation than we can cope with. It's like saying, "Lord, help us not to get involved in more temptation than we can handle." This interpretation, as I am sure you can see at once, makes good sense, and could well be what Jesus meant.

One of the biographers of Hudson Taylor, the intrepid missionary to China, tells how, in his early days in that land, Hudson Taylor met with several great disappointments. One day, after a spate of troubles, he took hold of a guide, who had demanded an outrageous fee from him, and shook him violently. A few hours later, he

realised he had denied his Lord by this action, and after searching his heart for the reason why he had succumbed to anger and violence, he realised that he had been so preoccupied with his problems that he had failed to commit his ways to the Lord. His biographer says, "If Hudson Taylor had prayed the prayer, 'Lead us not into temptation,' and committed his ways to the Lord, then perhaps the Spirit would have been able to direct his path so that he would not have faced more temptation than he could bear." It is an intriguing thought. But is it the fullest meaning of Jesus' words? Possibly – but I think it means much more, as we'll now see.

God's safety valve

Having looked at two different interpretations of the words "Lead us not into temptation", we come now to consider a third possible view, and one which I personally regard as the clearest meaning of our Lord's words. This interpretation was originally given by Chrysostom, an early Church father. He said, "This particular petition is the most natural appeal of human weakness as it faces danger. It's the cry of a heart that despises and abhors even the possibility of sin. It is the admission of human weakness, and a recognition of our human tendency to stumble on into folly."

Perhaps, in order to see these words of Chrysostom in a clear light, we need to set them against our Lord's experience in the Garden of Gethsemane. He prayed "My Father, if it be possible, let this cup pass from me" (Matt. 26:39). Jesus knew that the only way to accomplish redemption for the human race was by way of the Cross. Nevertheless, because He was human as well as divine, He gave expression to His humanity, even though, as the writer to the Hebrews said, He endured the Cross for the   Hebrews 12:2 joy that was set before Him.

You see, even though Jesus knew that the Cross had to be experienced in all its horror and torment, if men and women were to be redeemed, He still gave expression to His human feelings of dread and apprehension. Jesus did not feel guilty about this demonstration of His humanity, neither was God disappointed by His words, "Father, if it be possible, let this cup pass from me." The expression of our human weakness is a necessary part of prayer.

We could conclude from this then, that Jesus was providing a framework through which we could express our feelings of inadequacy and weakness, when faced with the possibility of temptation. One writer says of the words "Lead us not into temptation" – "They can only be properly understood when they are seen, not as cognitive [mental] but emotional." He meant that this statement of Jesus is not intended to be something that appeals to the mind, but something that appeals to the heart. It is as if Jesus is saying: "Even though your mind understands that

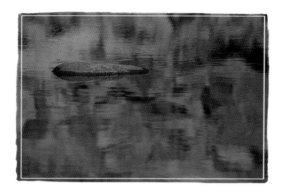

as you face temptation and overcome it, you become
stronger in God, there is still a part of you – your
emotions – that feels it would rather not face the
pressures. I understand this. I have been in that situation
myself. So I will provide a prayer framework for you that
will enable you to express, not so much your thoughts, but
your feelings. It will be an admission of your feelings of
weakness, but it will also be a release, for if your fears are
not expressed, they will be repressed, and will go
'underground' to cause trouble. So these words will
provide you with what you need – an opportunity to give
vent to your inner feelings of reluctance at facing
temptation."

   The more I ponder this, the more grateful I am to God
for recognising that I am not just an intellectual being but
an emotional being, and for building into His pattern of
prayer a safety valve that lets me express my inner feelings.
Rationally, I may perceive that temptation does a
perfecting work in my personality, yet in my feelings, if I
am honest, I would prefer not to face it. Our emotions, as
well as our intellect, are taken into consideration by our
Lord when laying down for us this pattern of prayer, for
He knows that to deny our feelings is to work against the
personality and not with it.

Psychologists tell us that the denial of feelings is the first step towards a nervous breakdown. Negative feelings must be handled carefully, for if repressed they are like the Chinese pirates of the past, who used to hide in the hold of a vessel, and then rise up when the ship was out on the open sea in order to attempt to capture and possess it. Then there was a fight.

One of the most fascinating and helpful insights I have ever found in my study of human personality is the fact that we don't have to act on our negative feelings, but we do have to acknowledge them. If we say with our minds: "Come on, temptation, I'm ready for you," and deny the fact that our emotions feel differently, then this pretence, that the feelings are not there, invites trouble into the personality. When, however, we acknowledge the feelings, and admit they are there, we rob them of their power to hurt us. I see this psychological mechanism wonderfully catered for in the words of Jesus which we are considering. They are the framework in which our feelings can have a vote also. Thus, though not acted upon, they are not denied.

We shall spend a few more moments considering the words "Lead us not into temptation, but deliver us from evil". We'll now concentrate on the last words of the statement – "deliver us from evil". Notice it is not a prayer for deliverance from this or that type of evil, but from evil itself. To Jesus, evil was evil in whatever form it came – whether in the evil of the flesh, the evil of the disposition, whether in the individual will or in the corporate will. Evil was never good, and good was never evil.

Someone has pointed out that the word "evil" is the word "live" spelt backwards. Evil, then, could be said to be anti-life. Non-Christians are finding out how not to live the hard way. They think they know better than God, and follow a way of their own choosing, only to find, like the rats in the scientific experiments who go down the wrong path, that there are wires at the end which carry electric shocks. These shocks are of various kinds: neuroses, inner conflicts, as well as some forms of physical illness.

Our health service has seen an explosion in its treatment of sexually transmitted diseases – a symptom of society's sexual permissiveness. God has made it impossible for us to live against His design, or harm ourselves without His protest. And He protests because He loves us. We can decide to have done with evil. The best way to deal with evil is to keep away from it, hence the prayer "Lead us not into temptation, but deliver us from evil." I say again, evil is bad for us, and good is good for us.

The Doxology

We come now to the final section of the Lord's Prayer: "For thine is the kingdom and the power and the glory, for ever. Amen." This part of Jesus' pattern of prayer – a doxology – is so beautiful that it somehow seems almost irreverent to try to dissect it. Some believe that Jesus did not actually say these words. They claim that they were added by someone else at a later date, which is why they are not included in some versions of the Bible. Some manuscripts have it, and some do not. I have looked long at the evidence for and against their inclusion in the sacred Scriptures, and I am perfectly satisfied myself that they were part of Jesus' original pattern of prayer.

The prayer ends, as it begins, with an assertion of God's majesty and glory "Thine is the kingdom". I believe that the emphasis here should be placed on the word "is", "Thine is the kingdom" – now. Despite all appearances to the contrary, God has never abdicated His position as ruler of the universe. What a heartening thought that is in these days, a thought to fill the soul with song, and flood the heart with hope and gladness. It is true that there are many things in the world that militate against His authority – war, poverty, unemployment, drink, gambling, social impurity, and so on. All these seem a flat and final refutation of the phrase "Thine is the Kingdom", but their days are numbered. The hour will come when the kingdoms of this world will signal their final surrender, and pledge their allegiance to their rightful Lord.

Despite all evidences to the contrary, God is in charge of the world's affairs – Our God reigns! The "power and the glory" spoken of here are Kingdom power and glory. The other type of power and glory, that which is measured by earthly standards alone, and rejected by Jesus in His temptation in the wilderness, is doomed to dissolution and decay. Ezekiel the prophet, speaking centuries ago of the impermanence of anything not founded on Kingdom values, said: "Your doom appears; your sin has blossomed, your pride has budded" (Ezek. 7:10, Moffatt). Note the steps: doom appears, sin blossoms and pride has budded. And the fruit of all this? Dissolution and decay.

I have spoken before of my fondness for Moffatt's translation, despite his astonishing liberties with some texts, but I know of nothing that excites me more than his translation of 2 Thessalonians 2:3. When speaking of a prominent figure, who will arise in the last days and challenge the authority of God's Kingdom, he refers to him as "the Lawless One, the doomed One". Those who are lawless, who break the laws of God's Kingdom, which are written into the very nature of things, are doomed. Perhaps not today, nor tomorrow, but inevitably anything that is against God's Kingdom is destined to destruction. It carries within itself the seeds of its own dissolution and decay.

2 Thessalonians 2:3

We are seeing that the final part of the Lord's Prayer, which (as we said) is really a doxology, contains a categorical assertion that God reigns through His Kingdom – now. It manifestly requires a measure of faith and courage to affirm that truth in our modern society, when so many things seem positively to shout against it – so many wrongs that clamour for redress, so many problems that demand a solution and so many social evils whose existence appear utterly incompatible with the reign of God. Yet affirm it, we must.

A dear Christian in a letter to me some time ago said: "I look around the world and am appalled. My only comfort is the hymn 'Jesus shall reign where'er the sun.' I, therefore, sit back and watch and wait the day." I told her that her letter reminded me of some words I heard someone put together in a conference once:

Sit down, O men of God!
His Kingdom He will bring,
Whenever it shall please His will.
You need not do a thing!

In my reply I said: "Yes, it's true that one day the Kingdom of God shall 'stretch from shore to shore', but let us not ignore the fact that God is reigning now. Given our consent and co-operation, the Almighty can greatly affect the world through our committed lives. If we fail to see this, then it is possible that we struggle and stumble through life, waiting for Him, while all the time He is waiting for us."

This lady, had indicated her intention to withdraw from life, and await the day when God would finally establish His Kingdom in power and glory on the earth. I replied with a parody of a hymn that apparently got her thinking.

She wrote back in a few weeks, and said: "You were right. I was waiting for God, but now I realise He is waiting for me." She ended her letter with the words of the hymn:

Rise up, O men of God!
Have done with lesser things;
Give heart and soul and mind and strength
To serve the King of kings.

This, not the parody I referred to, must indicate our line of action. Yes, of course, the final ushering in of God's Kingdom is yet to take place, but that does not mean that He is taking a back seat in the world's affairs. God wants to reign through us! We need not wait for the day when dramatically and spectacularly the great God of the universe demonstrates His imperial power. As through these closing pages, He sounds forth a rallying cry, respond to it, I urge you, with a fresh consecration of purpose, and dedicate yourself to letting Him reign through you.

Follow the King

We have been saying that when Jesus uttered the words – "For thine is the kingdom and the power and the glory, for ever. Amen" – it must be seen as an assertion of God's kingly rule – now. The Almighty has never abdicated His throne. He rules – and our task, as His followers, is to affirm this in our attitudes, our behaviour and in our daily living.

As we approach the end of our study in which we have been excavating the jewels of the Lord's Prayer, we must ask ourselves: what practical steps can we take to substantiate our assertion that God reigns now? Out of many possibilities, let me finish by just focusing on two.

We can do it by our lips. Even though so many ugly and obtrusive facts seem to militate against the truth, we must tell men and women that, behind the disordered events of this age, God is at work. We can do it also by our lives. The greatest contribution we can make individually to the world at this present time is to demonstrate, by our lives, that the King of heaven is reigning in us. High-principled, sacrificial and serviceable living is an irrefutable argument for the fact of God's rulership in the world. Tennyson put it in these words:

Follow the Christ – the King!
Live pure! Speak true! Right wrong!
Follow the King! Else wherefore born?

The best guarantee we can give to a sceptical world
that "blessings abound where'er He reigns", is that those
eminently desirable results have actually been achieved in
our own lives.

Amen – so be it!

Honesty compels me to admit that over this study my personal approach to prayer has undergone a complete overhaul, and I have brought my praying more in line with Jesus' pattern than ever before. After many years as a Christian, I am just waking up to what I have missed. Prayer to be effective must flow out of a truly committed heart: it must be the definition of our spirit, our attitude to God.

An unknown author put it this way: "I cannot say 'our' if I live only for myself. I cannot say 'Father' if I do not try to act like His child. I cannot say 'who art in heaven' if I am laying up no treasure there. I cannot say 'hallowed be thy name' if I am not striving for holiness. I cannot say 'Thy kingdom come' if I am not doing all in my power to hasten that event. I cannot say 'give us this day our daily bread' if I am dishonest, or seeking something for nothing. I cannot say 'forgive us our trespasses' if I bear a grudge against another. I cannot say 'lead us not into temptation' if I deliberately place myself in its path. I cannot say 'deliver us from evil' if I do not put on the armour of God. I cannot say 'thine is the kingdom and the power and the glory' if I do not give the King the loyalty due to Him from a faithful subject. And I cannot say 'for ever' if the horizon of my life is bounded completely by time."

The whole thrust of the Lord's Prayer is that when we give God His rightful place, He gives us our rightful place. But not before.

NATIONAL DISTRIBUTORS

UK (and countries not listed below): CWR, PO Box 230, Farnham, Surrey GU9 8EP. Tel: (01252) 784710 Outside UK (44) 1252 784710

AUSTRALIA: CMC Australasia, PO Box 519, Belmont, Victoria 3216. Tel: (03) 5241 3288

CANADA: CMC Distribution Ltd, PO Box 7000, Niagara on the Lake, Ontario L0S 1JO. Tel: (0800) 325 1297

GHANA: Challenge Enterprises of Ghana, PO Box 5723, Accra. Tel: (021) 222437/223249 Fax: (021) 226227

HONG KONG: Cross Communications Ltd, 1/F, 562A Nathan Road, Kowloon. Tel: 2780 1188 Fax: 2770 6229

INDIA: Crystal Communications, 10-3-18/4/1, East Marredpally, Secunderabad – 500 026. Tel/Fax: (040) 7732801

KENYA: Keswick Bookshop, PO Box 10242, Nairobi. Tel: (02) 331692/226047

MALAYSIA: Salvation Book Centre (M) Sdn Bhd, 23 Jalan SS 2/64, 47300 Petaling Jaya, Selangor. Tel: (03) 78766411/78766797 Fax: (03) 78757066/78756360

NEW ZEALAND: CMC New Zealand Ltd, Private Bag, 17910 Green Lane, Auckland. Tel: (09) 5249393 Fax: (09) 5222137

NIGERIA: FBFM, Helen Baugh House, 96 St Finbarr's College Road, Akoka, Lagos. Tel: (01) 7747429/4700218/825775/827264

PHILIPPINES: OMF Literature Inc, 776 Boni Avenue, Mandaluyong City. Tel: (02) 531 2183 Fax: (02) 531 1960

REPUBLIC OF IRELAND: Scripture Union, 40 Talbot Street, Dublin 1. Tel: (01) 8363764

SINGAPORE: Campus Crusade Asia Ltd, 315 Outram Road, 06-08 Tan Boon Liat Building, Singapore 169074. Tel: (065) 222 3640

SOUTH AFRICA: Struik Christian Books, 80 MacKenzie Street, PO Box 1144, Cape Town 8000. Tel: (021) 462 4360 Fax: (021) 461 3612

SRI LANKA: Christombu Books, 27 Hospital Street, Colombo 1. Tel: (01) 433142/328909

TANZANIA: CLC Christian Book Centre, PO Box 1384, Mkwepu Street, Dar es Salaam. Tel: (051) 2119439

UGANDA: New Day Bookshop, PO Box 2021, Kampala. Tel: (041) 255377

ZIMBABWE: Word of Life Books, Shop 4, Memorial Building, 35 S Machel Avenue, Harare. Tel: (04) 781305 Fax: (04) 774739

For e-mail addresses, visit the CWR web site: www.cwr.org.uk

Bible Classics

£4.99

An attractive and easy-to-read series exploring God's will for our lives, making us the people He has called us to be. These make wonderful gifts for friends and family.

The *23rd Psalm* presents one of the most encouraging and instructive passages from the Bible in a way that will inspire enquiring minds. *The Divine Gardener* shows how God is at work shaping our lives and *The Divine Eagle* illustrates how God sometimes pushes us out of our comfortable worlds towards a deeper faith in Him.

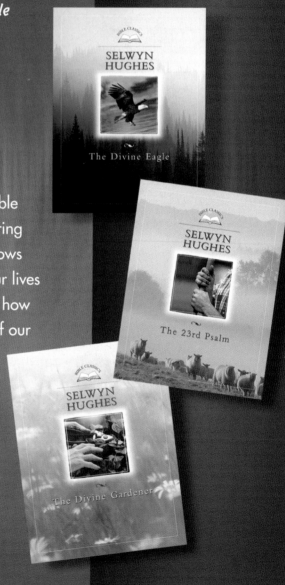

- **The Divine Eagle**
  ISBN 1–85345–190–8

- **The 23rd Psalm**
  ISBN 1–85345–192–4

- **The Divine Gardener**
  ISBN 1–85345–191–6